A Teaching Guide to

Island of the Blue Dolphins

by Mary F. Spicer

Illustration by Kathy Kifer and Dahna Solar

Dedicated to
Wendel Z. (Sam) Hall
1938-1994
A teacher's teacher—always a source of inspiration
and encouragement to me.

Island of the Blue Dolphins
Published by
Dell Publishing
(Reprinted by arrangement with Houghton Mifflin Company)
a division of
Bantam Doubleday Dell Publishing Group, Inc.
1540 Broadway
New York, New York 10036

Published by
Garlic Press
605 Powers St.
Eugene, OR 97402

ISBN 0-931993-79-2
Order Number GP-079

www.garlicpress.com

Table of Contents

NOTES TO THE TEACHER

The Discovering Literature Series is designed to develop a student's appreciation for good literature and to improve reading comprehension. While many skills reinforce a student's ability to comprehend what he or she reads (sequencing, cause and effect, finding details, using context clues), two skills are vital. They are: discerning **main ideas** and **summarizing** text. Students who can master these two essential skills develop into sophisticated readers.

The following discussion details the various elements that constitute this Series.

About Chapter Organization

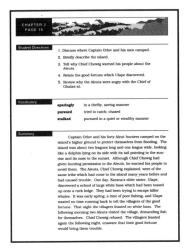

Sample: Chapter 2 with Student Directives, Chapter Vocabulary, and Chapter Summary.

Each chapter analysis is organized into three basic elements: **Student Directives**, **Chapter Vocabulary**, and **Chapter Summary**. Student Directives and Chapter Vocabulary need to be displayed on the board or on an overhead projector after each chapter is read. Students copy the Chapter Vocabulary and write their own summaries following the Student Directives.

The **Student Directives** contain the main ideas in each chapter. They provide the students, working individually or in groups, with a framework for developing their summaries. Student Directives can also be used as group discussion topics.

The **Chapter Vocabulary** includes definitions of key words from each chapter. To save time, students need only to copy, not look up, definitions. Suggestions for teaching vocabulary to students are as follows:

1. Make and display flashcards with the words and definitions. Refer to vocabulary cards in daily review.
2. Have students write sentences individually, in groups, or as a class using the words in the story's context.
3. Give frequent quizzes before an actual test.
4. Have students make their own vocabulary crossword puzzles or word search puzzles.
5. Play 20 questions with vocabulary words.
6. Host a vocabulary bee where the students give definitions for the word rather than spelling it.

A **Chapter Summary** for each chapter is included for teacher use and knowledge. Some students may initially need to copy the summaries in order to feel comfortable writing their own subsequent ones. Other students can use the completed summaries as a comparison to guide their own work. Summary

Sample:
Blackline Master

writing provides an opportunity to polish student composition skills, in addition to reading skills.

The **blackline master**, *Chapter Summary & Vocabulary*, is provided on page 73. It can be duplicated for student use. Teachers can also use it to make transparencies for displaying Student Directives and Chapter Vocabulary.

In addition, teachers may opt to have students make folders to house their Chapter Summary & Vocabulary sheets. A sample cover sheet (see page 74) for student embellishments has been provided. Cover sheets can be laminated, if desired, and affixed to a manila (or other) folder.

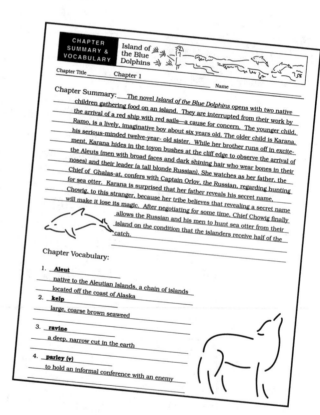

Sample Transparency:
Student Directives and Chapter Vocabulary

Sample Transparency:
Chapter Summary and Chapter Vocabulary

The above two samples serve to illustrate how the **blackline master**, *Chapter Summary & Vocabulary*, can be used as a transparency to focus student work. These transparencies are particularly effective for displaying Student Directives and Chapter Vocabulary. They are also effective for initially modeling how Chapter Summaries can be written.

About the Skill Pages

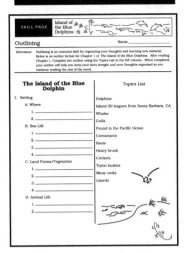

Sample: Skill Page

Skill Pages throughout the series have been developed to increase students' understanding of various literary elements and to reinforce vital reading skills. Since the entire series is devoted to reinforcing **main ideas** and **summarizing** skills, no further work has been provided on these skills. Depending upon each novel, Skill Pages reinforce various skills from among the following: **outlining**; **cause and effect**; **sequencing**; **character, setting, and plot development**; and **figurative language**. You will note that character development is based upon a values framework.

About the Tests

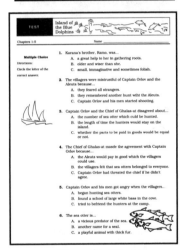

Sample: Test

At the end of each five-chapter block, a comprehensive open-book **Test** has been developed for your use. Each test includes reading comprehension, vocabulary, and short essays.

An Answer Key is provided at the back of the book for each Test.

The vocabulary portion of the Tests may be particularly difficult. You will probably want to give one or two vocabulary quizzes before administering each of the six Tests.

About the Writer's Forum

Sample: Writer's Forum

Suggestions for writing are presented under the **Writer's Forum** throughout this guide. You can choose from these suggestions or substitute your own creative-writing ideas.

Student Directives

1. Tell where the children were and what they sighted.

2. Briefly describe Ramo and Karana.

3. Briefly describe the Russian.

4. Tell about the discussion between Captain Orlov and Chief Chowig.

5. Review why Karana was surprised by her father.

6. Discuss the agreement between Captain Orlov and Chief Chowig.

Vocabulary

Aleut   native to the Aleutian Islands, a chain of islands located off the coast of Alaska

kelp   large, coarse brown seaweed

ravine   a deep, narrow cut in the earth

parley (v)   to hold an informal conference with an enemy

Summary

The novel *Island of the Blue Dolphins* opens with two native children gathering food on an island. They are interrupted from their work by the arrival of a red ship with red sails—a cause for concern. The younger child, Ramo, is a lively, imaginative boy about six years old. The older child is Karana, his serious-minded twelve-year old sister. While her brother runs off in excitement, Karana hides in the toyon bushes at the cliff edge to observe the arrival of the Aleuts (men with broad faces and dark shining hair who wear bones in their noses) and their leader (a tall blonde Russian). She watches as her father, the Chief of Ghalas-at, confers with Captain Orlov, the Russian, regarding hunting for sea otter. Karana is surprised that her father reveals his secret name, Chowig, to this stranger, because her tribe believes that revealing a secret name will make it lose its magic. After negotiating for some time, Chief Chowig finally allows the Russian and his men to hunt sea otter from their island on the condition that the islanders receive half of the catch.

Setting of *Island of the Blue Dolphins*   Name_____

The Author's Note at the end of *Island of the Blue Dolphins* provides the reader with some information about the location of Karana's island. The island was named San Nicolas Island, in honor of the patron saint of sailors and travelers. San Nicolas Island is located off the southern coast of California.

Alaska

Aleutian Islands

CANADA

The Aleuts who invaded Karana's island were people from the Aleutian Islands, a chain of islands extending from the Alaska peninsula in a southwesterly direction. The Aleuts, believed to be descendents of natives from the Alaskan mainland, earned their living primarily from hunting and fishing.

Because word spread to Russia about the excellent hunting on the Aleutian Islands, Russians came and dominated the native tribes in the 1800s. (Consult a globe or world map to see Russia's proximity to the Aleutian Islands.) The Russians did not treat the Aleuts well, and for a while, the Aleuts were on the verge of extinction. Today the Aleutian Islands, as well as Alaska, are part of the United States, and the Aleuts have full U.S. citizenship and preserve many of their old customs.

UNITED STATES

California

San Nicolas Island →

Directions: After carefully reading the above article about the Setting, match the terms on the left with the phrases on the right. Place the correct letter on each line.

_____ San Nicolas Island   A. Land which lay to the east of Karana

_____ California   B. Islands streaming from Alaska

_____ Aleutian Islands   C. The real name of Karana's island

_____ Russians   D. Territory near the Aleutian Islands

_____ Alaska   E. Country controlling the Aleutian Islands today

_____ United States   F. People who dominated the Aleuts

Outlining, Page 1

Name _____

Directions: Outlining is an essential skill for organizing your thoughts and learning new material. Below is an outline format for Chapter 1 of *Island of the Blue Dolphins*. After reading Chapter 1, complete the outline using the Topics List in the right column. When completed, your outline will help you keep your facts straight and your thoughts organized as you continue reading the rest of the novel.

Island of the Blue Dolphins

I. Setting

    A. Where

        1. _____

        2. _____

    B. Sea Life

        1. _____

        2. _____

        3. _____

        4. _____

        5. _____

    C. Land Forms/Vegetation

        1. _____

        2. _____

        3. _____

        4. _____

    D. Land Animals

        1. _____

        2. _____

Topics List

Dolphins

Island 20 leagues from Santa Barbara, CA

Whales

Gulls

Found in the Pacific Ocean

Cormorants

Roots

Heavy brush

Crickets

Toyon bushes

Many rocks

Lizards

Sea otter

Outlining, Page 2

Name_____

II. Characters

A. Karana

1. _____

2. _____

3. _____

B. Ramo

1. _____

2. _____

3. _____

C. Chief Chowig

1. _____

2. _____

3. _____

D. Captain Orlov

1. _____

2. _____

3. _____

4. _____

5. _____

Topics List

Serious

Playful

Chief of Ghalas-at

12 years old

Wanted to divide catch equally

Remembered another hunt

Looked at harbor as if it were his

Imaginative

Came to hunt sea otter

Observant

Claimed to come in peace

Did not want to divide catch equally

6 years old

Wanted to camp on island

III. Plot Prediction

Question: In every novel, there is a problem to overcome. Can you make a guess as to what the problem might be in this story?

_____

_____

_____

Student Directives

1. Discuss where Captain Orlov and his men camped.

2. Briefly describe the island.

3. Tell why Chief Chowig warned his people about the Aleuts.

4. Relate the good fortune which Ulape discovered.

5. Review why the Aleuts were angry with the Chief of Ghalas-at.

Vocabulary

league	a measure of distance equal to about three miles
sparingly	in a thrifty, saving manner
pursued	chased
stalked	walked stiffly or angrily

Summary

Captain Orlov and his forty Aleut hunters camped on the island's higher ground to protect themselves from flooding. The island was about two leagues long and one league wide and looked like a dolphin lying on its side with its tail pointing to the sunrise and its nose to the sunset. Although Chief Chowig had given hunting permission to the Aleuts, he warned his people to avoid them. The Aleuts, Chief Chowig explained, were of the same tribe which had come to the island many years before and had caused trouble. One day, Karana's older sister, Ulape, discovered a school of large white bass which had been tossed up onto a rock ledge. They had been trying to escape killer whales. It was early spring, a time of poor fishing, and Ulape wasted no time running back to tell the villagers of the good fortune. That night the villagers feasted on white bass. The following morning two Aleuts visited the village, demanding fish for themselves. Chief Chowig refused. The villagers feasted again the following night, unaware that their good fortune would bring them trouble.

Student Directives

1. Describe the sea otter which the Aleuts hunted.

2. Tell why Karana was angry.

3. Relate why the villagers kept watch on the Aleuts.

4. Review how the villagers knew that the Aleuts were preparing to leave.

Vocabulary

slain	killed; murdered
pelts	the skins of furry animals
strewn	covered by objects that are scattered or carelessly spread around
stunted	slowed in normal growth

Summary

The Aleuts continually hunted the sea otter, an animal which looks like a seal but has a shorter nose, small webbed feet, and thick beautiful fur. Of all the sea animals, the sea otter is the most playful. Karana, who loved the otter and considered them her friends, was very angry when she came out each morning to see the beach strewn with carcasses and the waves red with blood. The villagers kept a constant watch on the Aleuts, fearing that they would leave without paying their share. They watched carefully as the Aleut woman spent an afternoon cleaning her skin aprons and Captain Orlov trimmed his beard. These were indications to the villagers that the time for the Aleuts' departure was drawing near.

Student Directives

1. Discuss the argument between Captain Orlov and Chief Chowig.

2. Review the battle which took place on the island.

3. Tell why the villagers thought their chief had fallen.

Vocabulary

ceased	stopped; ended
bales	large bundles of material tied together
retreat (v)	withdraw; pull back

Summary

   As Captain Orlov and the Aleuts were packing their ship with otter pelts, Chief Chowig confronted them about their failure to pay their share. Raising his hand to give a signal, Captain Orlov commanded two hunters to bring a black chest filled with colored beads and offered it as payment. The Chief countered that one string of beads was not sufficient payment for one otter pelt. After arguing for some time about the number of chests needed to make payment for all the pelts, Captain Orlov, seeing a storm approaching, commanded his hunters to finish loading the ship. He refused to discuss further payment with the Chief. Before the villagers were even aware of how it had started, a fight began. The villagers, with their spears raised, rushed Captain Orlov and his men. At first, it seemed that the villagers would win, but Captain Orlov brought in more Aleuts and de-feated the villagers. As the Russian and the Aleuts left with their ship, the villagers ran crying to the beach to find their wounded and dead warriors. Karana's father, Chief of Ghalas-at, was among the dead. All the villagers agreed that he had weakened himself by having told Captain Orlov his secret name.

Student Directives

1. Discuss the effects of the battle on the village of Ghalas-at.

2. Review the naming of a new chief.

3. Tell about the new division of labor and the men's reaction to women as hunters.

4. Relate the real reason for unrest in the village.

5. Discuss Kimki's decision to explore a country to the east.

Vocabulary

portioned   cut or divided into portions or shares

abalones   large sea snails having a bowl-like shell

mesa   a flat-topped hill with steep sides

decreed   proclaimed; made an official order

Summary

The night following the battle was terrible for Ghalas-at; of the forty-two men in the tribe, only fifteen remained, and seven of those were old men. Every family had lost someone. The council chose a new chief, Kimki, who was very old, but had been a good hunter in his youth. Kimki gave new jobs to each villager, telling the women that they needed to become hunters to replace the men who had died. Realizing that survival depended on their efforts, the women worked so hard at hunting that the villagers actually fared better than when the hunting was done by men. Life in the village should have been peaceful, but it was not. The men were angry that the women had taken over tasks which were rightfully theirs. And so, Kimki once again decreed that the work would be divided—men would hunt and women would harvest. The real reason for unrest, however, was the unseen presence of all the men who had died at the cove. After much thought, Kimki decided that he alone would explore a country to the east, where he had been as a boy, to make a place for his village. As the villagers watched Kimki paddle his canoe across the sea, they wondered if they would ever see him again.

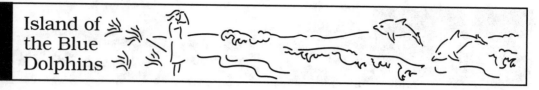
Multiple Choice

Directions:

Circle the letter of the correct answer.

1. Karana's brother, Ramo, was...
   A. a great help to her in gathering roots.
   B. older and wiser than she.
   C. small, imaginative, and sometimes foolish.

2. Chief Chowig was mistrustful of Captain Orlov and the Aleuts because...
   A. he feared all strangers.
   B. he remembered another hunt with the Aleuts.
   C. Captain Orlov and his men started shooting.

3. Captain Orlov and the Chief of Ghalas-at disagreed about...
   A. the number of sea otter which could be hunted.
   B. the length of time the hunters would stay on the island.
   C. whether the parts to be paid in goods would be equal or not.

4. The Chief of Ghalas-at made the agreement with Captain Orlov because...
   A. the Aleuts would pay in goods which the villagers could use.
   B. the villagers felt that sea otter belonged to everyone.
   C. Captain Orlov had threatened the Chief if he didn't agree.

5. Captain Orlov and his men got angry when the villagers...
   A. began hunting sea otter.
   B. did not share the white bass from the cove.
   C. tried to befriend the hunters at the camp.

6. The sea otter is...
   A. a vicious predator of the sea.
   B. another name for a seal.
   C. a playful animal with thick fur.

7. Karana warned her father about the hunters because she was...

    A. afraid that they would harm her or Ramo.

    B. worried that the hunters were spying on the villagers.

    C. afraid that the hunters were killing all the sea otter.

8. When the hunters were packing to leave, Chief Chowig felt that Captain Orlov was...

    A. trying to cheat him out of proper payment.

    B. being fair about paying his debt.

    C. going to leave some sea otter pelts as payment.

9. Captain Orlov was in a hurry to pack his ship because he...

    A. wanted to continue hunting in other places.

    B. saw storm clouds coming.

    C. was afraid of the villagers.

10. After the defeat at Ghalas-at, the villagers needed to...

    A. send out a canoe to find Captain Orlov.

    B. leave the island quickly.

    C. elect a new chief.

kelp	league	ceased
ravine	stalked	portioned
parley	pelt	mesa
	stunted	

Vocabulary

Directions:

Fill in the blank with

the correct word.

1. _____   stopped; ended

2. _____   large, coarse brown seaweed

3. _____   a measure of distance equal to about three miles

4. _____   a flat-topped hill with steep sides

5. _____   a deep, narrow cut in the earth

6. _____   walked stiffly or angrily

7. _____   to hold an informal conference with
                            an enemy

8. _____   slowed in normal growth

9. _____   cut or divided into portions or shares

10. _____   the skin of a furry animal

Essay Questions

Directions:

Answer in complete

sentences.

1. Tell why Scott O'Dell chose *Island of the Blue Dolphins* as
   the title of the novel.

   _____

   _____

   _____

2. After reading Chapter 1, you may have been able to predict
   that Captain Orlov and his men were going to cause trouble.
   Give at least two clues which indicate that the villagers would
   ultimately have trouble with the Aleuts.

   _____

   _____

   _____

3. Karana and other members of her tribe were highly superstitious people. Choose an example from the novel which sup-
   ports this claim.

   _____

   _____

   _____

Student Directives

1. Discuss the villagers' reaction when Kimki did not return.

2. Briefly review the plan if the Aleuts returned.

3. Tell what incident alarmed the tribe.

4. Relate Nanko's message.

Vocabulary

shrouded   covered or hid from sight

ponder   to consider carefully

stout   sturdy; strong

dunes   hills of sand formed by the wind

Summary

During the long days and months of Kimki's absence, the tribe grew increasingly afraid. Matasaip, who had been chosen to replace Kimki in his absence, worried about the return of the Aleuts. Knowing that their reduced numbers left them unable to stop the Aleuts, Matasaip developed a plan to flee if the Aleuts were sighted. The tribe hid canoes supplied with food and water at the rocky end of the island. One day a ship was sighted, and the tribe feared it was the return of the Aleuts. As they hastily prepared to abandon the island, the tribe learned from Nanko that the ship did not belong to the Aleuts but to white men who brought a message from Kimki. Kimki had sent the white men to bring his tribe to safety. Fearful but happy, the villagers prepared to leave the island.

Student Directives

1. Discuss the tribe's preparations to leave the island.

2. Briefly describe the ship and the waves.

3. Tell what happened to Ramo, and describe Karana's reaction to the news about Ramo.

4. Relate what happened once Karana was back on land.

Vocabulary

strode	walked with long steps
awl	a pointed tool for poking holes in leather or wood
beckoned	summoned with a movement
forlorn	sad; hopeless

Summary

When the villagers learned that they would have time to pack, each began filling baskets with items to take with them. Karana packed needles, an awl, a good scraping knife, cooking pots, and a box of earrings. The white men's ship, on which the villagers were to sail, was many times larger than the villagers' canoes. On the day of their departure, the sea was very rough. The ship pitched wildly, but the villagers were somehow able to get on board. After calling for Ramo, Karana frantically searched for him on board the ship, but to no avail. Against her wishes, Ramo had gone back to the village to get his spear. The captain feared the storm would dash the ship against the rocks, so he was unwilling to go back for Ramo. Karana flung herself into the sea despite the effort of tribe members to hold her back. When she reached the island, Karana found a for-lorn-looking Ramo holding his spear. All that bothered Karana was that her beautiful skirt of woven yucca fibers was ruined.

About the Characters

Name_____

Directions: Below is a Character Chart to help you organize the characters from the novel. Fill in whatever information is missing—either the character's name or a character summary.

| Kimki | Matasaip | Chief Chowig | Aleuts |
| Ulape | Ramo | Karana | Nanko |

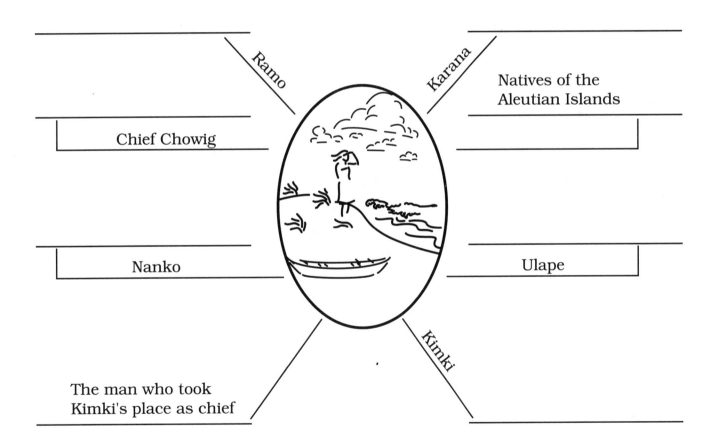

Ramo

Karana

Chief Chowig

Natives of the
Aleutian Islands

Nanko

Ulape

Kimki

The man who took
Kimki's place as chief

Student Directives

1. Review Karana's and Ramo's experiences those first days alone on the island.

2. Tell what was the children's greatest enemy.

3. Discuss Ramo's thoughts about living alone with Karana.

4. Relate Karana's reaction to her brother's death.

Vocabulary

gorged   ate fast and greedily

lair   living or resting place of a wild animal

mussels   bluish-black shellfish, somewhat like clams

Summary

After their reunion, Karana and Ramo set about making a life for themselves on the deserted island. The huts, looking like ghosts in the night light, reminded the children that they had to fend entirely for themselves. Packs of vicious wild dogs, searching for food, had become their dangerous enemies. Ramo, always playful and imaginative, enjoyed living alone with Karana. Since he was the son of a powerful chief, Ramo liked to pretend that he, too, was a powerful chief whose every command must be obeyed. Against Karana's better judgment, Ramo decided to visit the place where the canoes were hidden so that he could bring one back to their cove to use for fishing or travel. Karana awoke the following morning to discover that Ramo had left in the dark to go after the canoes. Rather than chasing after him, Karana gathered food and waited for his return. Karana became frightened after a time and went in search of Ramo. The barking of dogs led her to him. She discovered his lifeless body; he had been savagely attacked by the wild dogs. Karana kept vigil by her brother's body that night, silently vowing to kill each and every one of the wild dogs.

Student Directives

1. Discuss Karana's reactions to being stranded alone.

2. Review Karana's reason for moving to the rock.

3. Tell why Karana wouldn't make her own hunting weapons at first.

4. Review Karana's difficult decision to make her own weapons.

5. Relate Karana's reaction to the island's solitude.

Vocabulary

befell	happened to
sinews	tendons; the tissues fastening a muscle to a bone
crevices	cracks; narrow openings resulting from a split
pelicans	large fish-eating birds having a pouch under their beak

Summary

Karana was overcome by loneliness and desolation. Because the empty huts were a constant reminder to her of all that she had lost, Karana burned them, turning the village of Ghalas-at to ashes. Taking nothing but a basket of food, Karana chose a large rock on the headland overlooking Coral Cove. The rock was high enough to protect her from the vicious dogs while she slept, and it provided a storage area for food. Karana needed weapons for hunting and defense, but after searching the ruins and the chest left by the Aleuts, she decided she must make her own. The laws of Ghalas-at forbade women to make weapons, and Karana worried that a terrible fate might befall her if she disobeyed. With great difficulty, she defied the taboos and made her first spear, bow, and arrows. Her weapons gave her security, but she found little joy in her new life. The seasons passed, and still no ship came.

Elements of a Narrative

When an author creates a novel, a movie, or a television script, he or she must carefully plan a story which includes three basic elements: characters, setting, and plot. Simply stated, *somebody* has to be *somewhere* doing *something*. The author's story has merit if the characters are believable, engaging, and well developed. The setting(s) must be accurately described so that the reader can create a mental picture of it in his or her own mind. Specific details are vital in the development of a narrative; details make the story "come alive" for the reader.

Possibly the most complex narrative element is the plot. To develop the plot, the author must carefully plan a sequence of events which will hold the reader's or viewer's interest throughout the book, movie, or TV show. The author must concentrate on only the important aspects of the story so that it doesn't drag on. Additionally, the events must present a problem which the central character must resolve—either happily or unhappily.

Throughout the introductory chapter(s) or scene(s), the author must make these elements—characters, setting, and plot—clear to the reader or viewer. Using the introductory chapters as a guide, complete the following "Elements of a Narrative Outline" from *Island of the Blue Dolphins*.

Elements of a Narrative Outline

Name_____

Directions: Analyze the three basic elements of a narrative from your reading thus far in *Island of the Blue Dolphins.* Complete this outline for your analysis.

Main Character *(somebody)*   Describe the girl introduced in the first chapter.

A. _____

_____

B. _____

_____

C. _____

_____

Setting *(somewhere)*   Describe the setting where the story unfolds.

A. Where: _____

_____

B. When: _____

_____

Plot *(something)*   From your reading so far, predict how the plot (as a series of events) will be developed.

A. _____

_____

B. _____

_____

C. _____

_____

D. _____

_____

Student Directives

1. Discuss Karana's realization that no ship would be returning for her.

2. Relate how Karana weathered the fierce storm.

3. Explain Karana's decision to travel to the country to the east.

4. Briefly review Karana's troublesome voyage.

5. Tell about Karana's decision to return to the island.

Vocabulary

omen   a sign; a warning

chafing   rubbing

Summary

The seasons passed, and Karana realized that no ship would return for her. This reality caused Karana bitter loneliness, a deepening depression, and terrible dreams at night. One day a fierce storm blew in, and Karana had to move to the foot of her rock for protection. During the days and nights of the storm, while keeping a fire going to ward off the wild dogs, Karana decided to escape the island by canoe and to travel to the country to the east. She was able to free one small canoe from its secret place. Karana bravely embarked on her treacherous journey, taking only dried food and a basket of fresh water. By evening, Karana had paddled far from the island and could see nothing but ocean waves. To add to her problems, the canoe began leaking. She plugged the leaks with shreds from her skirt. Despite successfully plugging the leaks, Karana knew that the canoe's planks were weak and that they might rip open in rougher waves. Faced with the decision to travel on or to return to the deserted island, Karana finally realized that her only chance of survival was to go back to the island. As she turned around, a swarm of dolphins appeared. Karana knew that dolphins were an omen of good luck. Her spirits lifted somewhat, and she didn't feel so lonely as she returned, exhausted, to her island.

Sequencing

Name _____

Event 1: Children spot Aleut ship. _____

_____

Event 2: _____

_____

Event 3: _____

_____

Event 4: _____

_____

Event 5: Aleuts and islanders battle. _____

_____

Event 6: _____

_____

Event 7: _____

_____

Event 8: _____

_____

Event 9: _____

_____

Event 10: Ramo killed by wild dogs. ____

_____

Event 11: _____

_____

Event 12: _____

_____

Directions:

Using the timeline provided, sequence the following events from Chapters 1-10. Three events have been done for you.

- Kimki elected new chief.
- Karana jumps from ship.
- Children spot Aleut ship.
- Karana makes weapons.
- Aleuts and islanders battle.
- Ramo killed by wild dogs.
- Argument about dividing catch.
- Karana tries to flee.
- Captain Orlov leaves without paying.
- White men's ship arrives.
- Sea otter slaughtered.
- Ramo runs to get spear.

Multiple Choice

Directions:

Circle the letter of the

correct answer.

1. The villagers decided that if the Aleuts were to return to the island, they would...

    A. fight them off before they could land on the island.

    B. flee the island in canoes.

    C. hide in a secret part of the island.

2. The ship which Nanko spotted was carrying...

    A. Aleuts who had come to hunt sea otter.

    B. Kimki and some men from another tribe.

    C. some white men who were sent by Kimki.

3. Ulape, Karana's older sister, drew a thin mark with blue clay across her face because...

    A. she thought it made her look attractive.

    B. it was a sign that she was unmarried.

    C. it meant that she was engaged to Nanko.

4. While the villagers were boarding the huge ship, Ramo ran back to the village because he...

    A. had forgotten his spear.

    B. had left his pet lizard behind.

    C. wanted to get his toys.

5. The ship would not go back for Ramo because...

    A. it was already overcrowded.

    B. the villagers did not care about him.

    C. it would have been driven on the rocks.

6. When Karana and Ramo were stranded on the island, their most serious problem was...

    A. finding food and fresh water to drink.

    B. a pack of wild dogs roaming the island.

    C. a feeling of loneliness and despair.

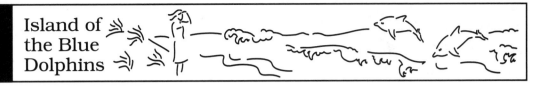
7. While stranded on the island, Ramo left the hut he shared with Karana because he wanted to...

    A. hunt for some mussels for breakfast.

    B. search the sea for a large ship to save them.

    C. go to the place where the canoes were hidden.

8. At first, Karana did not make her own weapons because...

    A. Ghalas-at laws prohibited women from doing so.

    B. she did not have the proper materials.

    C. she found all the spearheads she needed in the black chest left by the Aleuts.

9. Karana found help with directions at sea by...

    A. watching the location of familiar stars.

    B. using a map made by her people.

    C. remembering Kimki's advice about getting to the country to the east.

10. Karana decided to return to the island when she...

    A. found that her canoe was leaking.

    B. couldn't figure out which direction to follow.

    C. realized that the canoe planks might split in rough seas.

Vocabulary

Directions:

Fill in the blank with

the correct word.

ponder	forlorn	crevice
strode	gorged	omen
beckoned	dunes	chafing
	befell	

1. _____ happened to

2. _____ sad; hopeless

3. _____ a sign; a warning

4. _____   to consider carefully

5. _____   rubbing

6. _____   walked with long steps

7. _____   a crack; an opening

8. _____   ate fast and greedily

9. _____   summoned with a movement, as a
                           wave or a nod

10. _____   hills of sand formed by the wind

Essay Question

Directions:

Answer in complete

sentences.

The tribe to which Karana belonged was superstitious; that is, they believed that supernatural powers were attached to chance events, charms, or taboos. Give two examples of superstitious beliefs from the novel. You may use any chapter you have read so far.

_____

_____

_____

_____

_____

_____

_____

_____

_____

Student Directives

1. Discuss Karana's return to her island.

2. Review Karana's decision to build a house.

3. Discuss the problem of the wild dogs' lair.

4. Tell about the sea elephants' influence on Karana.

5. Explain Karana's feelings of good omen.

Vocabulary

brackish   having a salty taste, as of the sea

clamor   an uproar; a loud sound of shouting and confusion

Summary

Karana was surprised by her feelings of happiness as she returned to her island. Knowing that she would never again attempt to go to the country which lay to the east, Karana set about deciding on a location for a permanent home. She knew that she needed a place sheltered from the wind, not too far from Coral Cove, and close to a good spring. There were two such places—one was on the headland, and the other, less than a league to the west, was unfortunately near the wild dogs' lair. At the west location, Karana would first need to kill off all the wild dogs. Karana found that the spring water to the west was less brackish, and the location provided fairly good wind protection and visibility. The sea elephants, however, were the deciding factor for the location of the house. Even though their clamor was deafening, Karana loved to watch the noisy sea creatures playing along the shore. After two days of rain, Karana finally set out to gather the building materials she needed. The bright, sweet-smelling morning, fresh from the recent rain, made Karana feel that the day was an omen of good fortune.

Cause and Effect

Name _____

Directions: On the left is a list of causes. On the right is a list of effects. Match the correct effect with its cause by placing the correct letter in the blank.

A **Cause** produces a result.	An **Effect** results from a cause.

1. Because the Russians and the Aleuts had cheated Karana's tribe in the past, ____

2. In order to get the goods the Aleuts traded, ____

3. Chief Chowig feared that Captain Orlov might leave without paying, so ____

4. As a result of the women working very hard at hunting, ____

5. There were many bitter memories at Ghalas-at, so ____

6. When Ulape drew a blue mark across her nose and cheekbone, ____

7. In order to have weapons for protection, ____

8. Because Karana wanted to make spear points from its teeth, ____

9. Because Karana felt that the dolphins were animals of good omen, ____

10. Since Karana liked the noise and clamor of the sea elephants, ____

A. she let people know that she was unmarried.

B. seeing them made her feel happy about returning to her island.

C. the villagers actually had more food than when the men had hunted.

D. Kimki went exploring for a new place to settle.

E. she built her house near the cliffs where they played.

F. the tribe feared the arrival of the Aleut ship.

G. she wished to capture a sea elephant.

H. Chief Chowig finally agreed to let the Aleuts hunt the sea otter.

I. Karana defied a taboo against women making their own weapons.

J. he spent each night carefully working on a new spear.

Student Directives

1. Tell how Karana made her fence and house.

2. Describe what Karana ate and how she cooked.

3. Review Karana's preparations for killing the wild dogs.

Vocabulary

gruel   a thin porridge

sea elephant a sea animal of the seal family with long tusks, flippers, and a tough hide

Summary

Karana needed to make a fence for storage so that the wild animals would not be able to steal her food supply. Karana made a fence from the ribs of two whales that had washed up on the beach many years before. She wove many strands of bull kelp to hold the ribs in place. After completing the fence, she began to build her house, searching many days for poles to build the framework. Karana bound the roof poles together with sinew and covered them with broad leaves of female kelp. She then began to make her own utensils from stones and her cooking baskets from reeds and pitch. So that she would have a fire for cooking and heat, Karana dug out a fireplace and lined it with rocks. For food storage, she cut out cracks from the rock wall at the back of her house and kept food stored there. By winter's end, Karana had a warm comfortable house where she could cook anything she wished to eat. She now began making plans to kill the wild dogs. She spent many nights making weapons by the light of the *sai-sai* fish. Karana realized that she needed the tooth of a bull sea elephant to make a proper spear point. How she would kill a sea elephant was her next challenge.

Student Directives

1. Discuss Karana's fear as she prepared to hunt the bull sea elephant.

2. Briefly describe the sea elephants.

3. Tell about the attack by the young bull sea elephant.

4. Discuss Karana's injury.

5. Briefly tell how the battle between the two sea elephants progressed.

Vocabulary

wary   cautious; careful to avoid danger or difficulty

grating   making an unpleasant, harsh, scraping noise

rival   a person or opponent that competes with or tries to be better than the other

Summary

The night before Karana went to the place of the sea elephants, she did not sleep. Karana, worrried by her tribe's taboos against women making weapons, feared that she would be killed or injured during the hunt. The place where the sea elephants lived was lined with many cows and babies. The bull sea elephants, bad-tempered and jealous by nature, sat alone. Sea elephants are ugly animals with rough cracked-looking skin and a nose with a large hump. While Karana carefully watched the sea elephants, she saw one young bull elephant invade the territory of an old battle-scarred bull. A bloody fight began with the young bull holding on to the older bull's neck. The older bull broke loose and beat a hasty retreat directly towards Karana, causing her to fall and hurt her leg. A fearful battle ensued, and the sea was soon red with blood. Karana left to go home, needing to tend to her injury. As she was leaving, the young bull elephant had once again caught the throat of the old bull and proceeded into ferocious battle.

Student Directives

1. Briefly discuss Karana's injury.

2. Describe Karana's encounter with the wild dogs.

3. Tell about Karana's story in the cave.

4. Describe what Karana found when she returned to the sea elephants' place.

Vocabulary

lobe   a round part that protrudes or is otherwise set apart

venturing   approaching in the face of danger

basins   deep bowls that can hold a lot of liquid

Summary

By the time Karana returned home, her leg was badly swollen. She did not go out for five days. Karana had plenty of food to eat, but she ran low on water. It became necessary for her to go to the ravine. Carrying food and weapons on her back, Karana had to crawl to the spring. While resting along the way, Karana was spotted by the big gray leader of the wild dogs. Slowly making her way to the spring, Karana felt the dogs' eyes following her. When she arrived at the spring, she drank freely and filled her water basket. She took refuge in a cave, fearing the dogs were waiting for her. This cave had been used by Karana's ancestors, who had carved figures of birds, sea creatures, and land animals along the walls. She stayed in the cave for six days. While there, she decided to make the cave her second home in case she should get sick again. When she felt better, Karana visited the sea elephants' place. She found the old bull elephant had been killed. She took the teeth she needed for spears. Soon she would be ready to go to the dogs' cave and kill them.

Student Directives

1. Discuss briefly the leader of the wild dogs.

2. Describe Karana's hunting tactics.

3. Tell about Karana's nursing the big gray dog.

4. Discuss what happened on the fourth day.

Vocabulary

bolder   showing more courage; less afraid

carcass   the body of any dead animal

Summary

Karana studied the leader of the wild dogs even more carefully than before and concluded that he must have been brought by the Aleuts. He was larger than the island dogs, and his hair was thicker. Because of his leadership, all the dogs had grown bolder. Karana had finally made enough weapons to begin killing off the wild dogs, and she set out for their lair. She piled brush near the mouth of the lair and set fire to it, hoping to smoke the dogs out. Karana waited and saved her arrows for the leader. When he finally came out, she shot an arrow into his chest. Wounded, the leader wandered off into the brush. Karana went home as night fell. She waited two rainy days before searching for the leader dog. She found him near death and could easily have killed him. Instead, she carried him home and nursed him for several days. After four days, the leader dog wagged his tail when Karana entered the house. She then gave her dog a name—Rontu, which meant Fox Eyes.

Multiple Choice

Directions:

Circle the letter of the correct answer.

1. When Karana returned from her attempted voyage to the country to the east, she felt...
    A. determined to fix her canoe and try the voyage again.
    B. unhappy at returning to the island.
    C. filled with happiness.

2. The main reason that Karana chose the site for her new home was that it...
    A. was located far away from the wild dogs' lair.
    B. was a place near the sea elephants.
    C. had higher rocks than those on the headland.

3. To make the fence which would surround her house, Karana used...
    A. wooden poles from trees.
    B. piled-up brush.
    C. whale ribs.

4. In order to make a good spear, Karana needed...
    A. the tusk like teeth of a bull sea elephant.
    B. the bone from a whale.
    C. spearheads from the Aleuts.

5. When Karana observed the bull sea elephants, she noticed that they...
    A. played freely with the cows and babies.
    B. only played with other bull sea elephants.
    C. sat alone because they are bad-tempered.

6. The old bull sea elephant attacked the younger one because...
    A. he liked to fight other bull sea elephants.
    B. the younger bull was going after the cows in the old bull's herd.
    C. the younger bull had attacked him first.

7. When Karana was injured, she finally had to crawl out of her house because she...

    A. had run out of food.

    B. had run out of water.

    C. was getting restless being cooped up.

8. When the dogs split up to encircle the injured Karana, she...

    A. took refuge in a cave.

    B. began shooting the dogs with her bow and arrows.

    C. ran for home.

9. To coax the dogs from their lair, Karana...

    A. left out bowls of red meat.

    B. set fire to some brush at the cave's entrance.

    C. called to them.

10. When Karana finally found the leader of the wild dogs, she...

    A. shot arrows into his body.

    B. gave him some water.

    C. took him home and nursed him.

---

brackish	wary	venturing
clamor	grating	bolder
gruel	rival	carcass
	lobe	

Vocabulary

Directions:

Fill in the blank with

the correct word.

1. _____　　making an unpleasant, harsh, scraping noise

2. _____　　the body of a dead animal

3. _____　　a person or opponent that competes or tries to be better than the other

4. _____   having a salty taste

5. _____   approaching in the face of danger

6. _____   an uproar, a loud sound of shouting
                              and confusion

7. _____   a rounded part that protrudes or is
                              set apart

8. _____   cautious; careful to avoid danger

9. _____   a thin porridge

10. _____   showing more courage; less afraid

Essay Questions

Directions:

Answer in complete

sentences.

1. Once Karana returned to her island after her brief venture to
   the country to the east, Karana was very organized in her
   approach to building a new life. Give four steps which Karana
   took to make her life better.

   _____

   _____

   _____

   _____

   _____

2. When Karana found the wounded leader dog with the arrow
   still lodged in his chest, she could have killed him on the spot.
   Why do you suppose that she chose to carry him home and
   nurse him instead?

   _____

   _____

   _____

   _____

   _____

Student Directives

1. Discuss Karana's canoe and her constant searching of the sea.

2. Tell why Karana was not lonely.

3. Review the discovery Karana made while she was canoeing.

4. Briefly describe the devilfish.

5. Tell what Karana would have to do to catch a devilfish.

Vocabulary

roost (v)   to rest or sleep, as on a perch

devilfish   (octopus) a sea animal that has a soft body and eight long arms covered with suckers

Summary

Karana constantly scanned the sea as she worked, searching for the white men's ship or the red ship of the Aleuts. In case the Aleuts came, Karana knew that she must be able to flee. Thus, she began working again on her canoe, making it smaller and filling the leaks with pitch. With Rontu as her faithful companion, Karana was no longer lonely. She spoke to him constantly, just as if he understood all that she said. When Karana had finished working on her canoe, she and Rontu took a long voyage, exploring the island's sea caves. One cave had a wide shelf of rock extending out to the sea. Karana knew that she had made a great discovery when she saw that the cave's back entrance joined the cliff below her house on the headland. This was just the place she needed to hide her canoe. Near the cave, Rontu became entranced with the movement of a large devilfish, a dangerous sea creature with bulging eyes and many arms. Since devilfish was the best food in the sea, Karana attempted to spear it, but the creature, shooting out a black liquid, escaped from her view. To spear a devilfish, Karana would need to work on a special kind of spear.

Student Directives

1. Briefly discuss how Karana made the devilfish spear.

2. Discuss Rontu's departure and battle with the dogs.

3. Tell why Karana chose not to shoot the attacking dogs.

4. Describe Rontu's trick to lure the dogs into attacking.

5. Describe Rontu's action after winning the fight with both dogs.

Vocabulary

barbed   having a sharp point or edge sticking backward from another point, as on a fishhook

heed (n)   attention

haunches   the upper legs, including the hips

lure   something that attracts or tempts

Summary

Karana worked on her spear during the rainy season. She was ready to hunt the giant devilfish the first day of spring. Rontu had been acting strangely and did not join her on the hunt. Returning from the beach with her small catch, she heard the distant sounds of dogs fighting. As she came to a meadow at the edge of a low cliff, Karana spotted Rontu with a half-circle of wild dogs facing him. Two dogs, their muzzles wet with blood, were preparing to attack Rontu—the remaining dogs were there to pounce upon the loser. Karana knew that she could easily shoot the attacking dogs with her bow and arrows, but she decided to let Rontu fight his own battle. To lure the dogs into attacking him, Rontu pretended to veer his eyes from the dogs and lick his wounds. Falling for Rontu's trick, the two dogs approached. Rontu leapt at the closer one, breaking the animal's foreleg with his bite. The spotted dog rushed at Rontu, slashing him on the flank. Lying on the grass, Rontu lured the spotted dog to him and grabbed the dog's throat in his jaws. After the attack had ended, Rontu walked to the mound where he gave a long howl. The wild dogs divided into two packs, never again to return to the headland.

Student Directives

1. Briefly describe the island's spring beauty.

2. Discuss Karana's pet birds.

3. Tell how Karana kept her birds from flying away.

4. Briefly describe Karana's "dress-up" clothes.

Vocabulary

singed   burned slightly, especially hair or feathers

Summary

Spring burst forth with an abundance of beautiful flowers and colorful, chattering birds. A pair of birds with yellow bodies and scarlet heads, which Karana had never seen before, made a nest near her house. The mother bird hatched two ugly gray babies from her speckled eggs. Taking the babies from their nest, Karana placed them in a cage made of reeds. After all the other birds would fly to the north, Karana would have these two as pets. The birds soon grew beautiful like their parents and began to sing the same songs. To keep her birds from flying away, Karana clipped their wings. She named them Tainor and Lurai. During the time she was taming the birds, Karana made herself another skirt of yucca fibers, a sealskin belt, and sandals. With her new clothes and a wreath of flowers in her hair, she walked along the cliff with Rontu and looked at the sea.

Student Directives

1. Discuss Karana's food-gathering techniques.

2. Tell why Karana avoided hunting when starfish were feeding.

3. Describe Karana's battle with the devilfish.

Vocabulary

prey (v)   to seize animals for food

flailing   waving or swinging something about

Summary

Karana spent one year searching for the giant devilfish, but she couldn't find it. She gave up her search and began gathering food and supplies for winter. While gathering abalones, she spotted the giant devilfish swimming in the clear water. Using her special spear, Karana tried for the devilfish. When the barbed point came loose, she knew that she had struck it, and a fierce battle ensued. The string from Karana's spear tightened in her hands, causing them to bleed. Karana finally pulled the devilfish onto the beach. Rontu rushed to seize it, but the devilfish was too heavy and three of its arms wound around him. Rontu was in trouble. Karana drove her whalebone knife into the devilfish. As she did, Karana felt as though countless leeches were sucking at her body. Slowly her pain lessened and the devilfish stopped moving. Too exhausted to drag the devilfish from the water, Karana walked home with many cuts and bruises on her body. After the encounter, she gave up attempting to spear giant devilfish.

Student Directives

1. Discuss Karana's preparations for winter.

2. Describe Karana's journey to the Black Cave.

3. Tell about Karana's reaction to the Aleut ship.

Vocabulary

shaft   a long, slender opening

Summary

Karana continued drying abalones for winter, hanging their colorful shells to keep the gulls away. She also caught small fish in a net, hanging them to dry for winter light. Rontu and Karana had taken many voyages that summer, one of which was to Black Cave. Located near the place where the canoes were stored, Black Cave proved to be a fearsome place. As Rontu and Karana entered the cave in their canoe, they saw a row of strange figures standing on a deep ledge. They were tall, with glittering eyes. Their arms and legs and short bodies were made of reeds and were clothed in gull feathers. Seated in the middle was a skeleton playing a flute, most certainly one of Karana's ancestors. Karana forgot that the tide was coming in, and she was unable to get out through the narrow entrance, so they had to spend the night in the cave. She paddled out of the cave with the first light, vowing never to return. One day, after Karana and Rontu had returned from Tall Rock, they saw the Aleut ship. Karana, after packing her pets, clothes, utensils, and baskets, went back to the headland to watch the Aleuts. Knowing that they would not come ashore in the dark, Karana had plenty of time to take her things to the cave and to make her house look as if no one lived there. She watched as the Aleuts brought their goods ashore and noticed an Aleut girl cooking over a fire. Being careful to leave no tracks, Karana and Rontu entered their dark cave and slept all day.

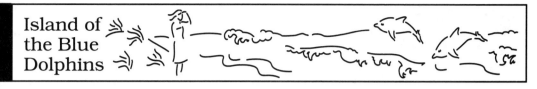

TEST

Island of
the Blue
Dolphins

Name _____

Multiple Choice

Directions:

Circle the letter of the

correct answer.

1. The most important reason that Karana needed a canoe was to...

   A. sail around the island with Rontu.

   B. use it for catching fish.

   C. use it for escape if the Aleuts came.

2. Karana was not lonely on her island because she...

   A. preferred solitude.

   B. had Rontu to talk to.

   C. knew that someone would be coming for her soon.

3. The devilfish are dangerous because they...

   A. squirt a black poisonous liquid at their enemy.

   B. have poisonous suckers on their arms.

   C. can wrap their arms around you and drown you.

4. Rontu lured the dogs into attacking by...

   A. pretending not to see them while licking his wounds.

   B. barking and growling at them.

   C. casually walking away into the bushes.

5. After Rontu's victory over the two attacking dogs, he...

   A. went immediately to Karana so that she would pet him.

   B. walked to the mound and gave a long howl.

   C. went back to the wild dogs' lair.

6. Karana clipped the wings of her caged birds because she...

   A. thought it would help them fly better.

   B. thought it made their wings more attractive.

   C. didn't want them to fly away.

7. After Karana killed the devilfish, she...

    A. dragged its body from the water.

    B. went home to go to sleep.

    C. cut off its many long arms.

8. When Karana entered the Black Cave, she knew that she...

    A. had found a perfect hiding place for her canoe.

    B. would visit there often.

    C. had found some of her ancestors.

9. When Karana saw the ship from the top of the cliff, she...

    A. thought it was the Aleuts because the ship came from the north.

    B. thought the ship belonged to white men from the east.

    C. had no idea to whom the ship belonged.

10. After the Aleuts landed, Karana...

    A. stayed in her house behind the whale rib fence.

    B. went to the headland to live.

    C. went to her cave by the ravine.

Vocabulary

Directions:

Fill in the blank with the correct word.

roost	heed	prey
devilfish	haunches	flailing
barbed	lure	shaft
	singed	

1. _____   upper part of legs, including the hips

2. _____   waving or swinging something about

3. _____   a sea animal that has a soft body and eight long arms covered with suckers

TEST

Island of
the Blue
Dolphins

Chapters 16-20, Page 3

Name _____

4. _____   to seize animals for food

5. _____   to rest or sleep, as on a perch

6. _____   burned slightly, especially hair or feathers

7. _____   having a sharp point or edge sticking backward, as on a fishhook

8. _____   a long, slender opening

9. _____   something that attracts or tempts

10. _____ attention

Essay Questions

Directions:

Answer in complete

sentences.

1. When Karana saw that Rontu was cornered by the pack of wild dogs, she decided not to kill his attackers. What was Karana's reasoning about refusing to help her pet dog?

_____

_____

_____

_____

_____

2. When Karana found the devilfish floating in the clear water below the edge of the reef, she decided to attack him. Explain how Karana and Rontu worked together to kill the devilfish.

_____

_____

_____

_____

_____

Student Directives

1. Discuss which one of the Aleuts Karana feared.

2. Review how Karana spent her time in the cave.

3. Briefly describe Karana's encounter with the Aleut girl.

4. Tell about Tutok's gift to Karana.

Vocabulary

giddy   silly; light hearted or foolish

Summary

As Karana stood watching the fire made by the Aleuts, she knew she had only one to fear—the girl. The men hunted all day. They would not discover her, but the girl easily could. The days that Karana and Rontu spent in the cave were long and tedious. Fearing that Rontu might not come back, Karana did not let him out unless she was with him. To keep herself amused, Karana began making a beautiful skirt from cormorant feathers. She burnt small fish for light in the cave. One day while Karana was outside admiring her skirt with the shimmering feathers, the Aleut girl chanced to see her. Karana could easily have killed the girl with her spear, but did not. Hesitantly, the two girls exchanged a few words, but mostly they gestured. They couldn't speak each other's language. The Aleut girl told Karana that her name was Tutok, but Karana did not trust Tutok enough to reveal her own name. After Tutok left, Karana prepared to change her location. Returning to the cave for the last two baskets she had planned to hide near her house, Karana felt that someone had been there. Looking down on the flat rock in front of her cave, Karana saw a necklace of black stones—a type of stone that Karana had never seen.

Student Directives

1. Discuss Karana's reaction to the necklace.

2. Describe how Karana and Tutok communicated.

3. Discuss the gift Karana made to Tutok.

4. Explain Karana's feelings when Tutok left.

Vocabulary

prow   the forward part of a boat or ship

Summary

At first, Karana would not take Tutok's necklace, but she kept eyeing it, wondering how many loops the necklace would make around her neck. Tutok appeared again at the cave. She looked about hesitantly for Karana, then started to leave. Karana suddenly ran out calling Tutok's name. Because Karana needed human companionship, she and Tutok became friends, teaching each other words from their own native language. Karana did not tell Tutok her secret name at first. Instead, Karana told her the name Won-a-pa-lei, The Girl with the Long Black Hair. Several days later, Karana told Tutok her secret name. Since Tutok had been so generous to her, Karana wanted to make her something in return. Karana set about making a circlet for Tutok's hair from abalone shells that had been flaked into disks, and ten tiny olivella shells. Karana presented her gift, to the delight of Tutok. The girls' visits increased and their friendship grew. Then one day Tutok no longer came. Finding it difficult to accept the loss of her friend, Karana pretended that Tutok would be arriving soon. After Tutok left, the island seemed very quiet.

Student Directives

1. Discuss Karana's reaction to the many sea otter left on the beach.

2. Tell about the one otter Karana befriended.

3. Review how Karana felt when Mon-a-nee left the pool.

4. Tell why this winter was difficult for Karana.

5. Discuss Karana's winter activities.

Vocabulary

reproachfully   in a scolding manner

smelt   small fish having oily flesh

Summary

The Aleuts left the beach strewn with many wounded sea otter. Karana killed the wounded ones with her spear because they were suffering. One young otter, though, was not badly hurt. Karana took it to a calm, shallow tide pool and fed it in the hope that it might recover. Karana brought fish every day for the otter and finally named it Mon-a-nee, which meant Little Boy with Large Eyes. At one point, Karana was not able to fish for Mon-a-nee for three days because the waves were too high. When she was able to return, she found that he had swum out into the ocean. Karana felt bad that Mon-a-nee had left, for she knew she would never be able to recognize him from the others. The winter after the Aleuts came was difficult for Karana because she had not been able to catch the little smelt and dry them to use for winter light. Since her nights were dark, Karana went to bed early. During the day, she made string for fishing gear, hooks of abalone shell, and earrings to match the necklace Tutok had given her. On sunny days, Karana would wear her cormorant dress with the necklace and earrings, and walk along the cliff with Rontu. She missed Tutok and would have imaginary conversations with her.

Student Directives

1. Discuss Tainor's and Lurai's nest.

2. Briefly describe the yard at Karana's house.

3. Review Karana's thoughts about Tutok and Ulape.

4. Describe Karana's reunion with Mon-a-nee.

5. Tell about Karana's decision regarding animals.

Vocabulary

fledglings	young birds
teetering	standing or walking unsteadily
reef	a ridge of sand or rock just about even with the surface of the water

Summary

When spring came again, Tainor and Lurai, Karana's birds, built a nest of dry seaweed and leaves and hair from Rontu's back. They hatched two ugly fledglings which would soon become beautiful birds. Karana gave them names and clipped their wings. Soon they were as tame as their parents. Karana's yard was filled with the happy sound of birds: Tainor, Lurai, the two fledglings, and a white gull which had injured its leg. Sometimes, though, Karana did feel loneliness, remembering Tutok and her sister, Ulape. She wondered if Ulape was married and had children. That spring, while Karana was paddling in her canoe, one sea otter came ashore, following her. She felt certain that the otter was Mon-a-nee. A few months later, the otter came back and Karana was delighted to see two baby sea otter accompanying it. Karana thought it better to change the otter's name to Won-a-nee, Girl with the Large Eyes. After that summer, Karana had so many animal friends that she decided never to kill another animal, for without them "the earth would be an unhappy place."

Student Directives

1. Discuss the change in the summer habits of the sea otter.

2. Tell Karana's reaction to the passing of time.

3. Describe Rontu's death and burial.

Vocabulary

quiver (n)   a case for holding arrows

urged   encouraged; pushed or forced

Summary

For many summers after the Aleuts had left, the sea otter did not remain at Coral Cove. Only after all the otter that remembered the hunt had died did the young sea otter stay for the summer at Coral Cove. Ever since her brother, Ramo, had died, Karana had kept track of all the months that she had spent on the island—marking notches on a pole beside her door. But after Rontu died, the months had little meaning and Karana only counted the seasons; she eventually stopped marking those as well. In the weeks before he died, Rontu no longer joined Karana to hunt for fish. One night Rontu did not return home, and Karana anxiously went looking for him. She found him at last at the back of a cave. Karana sat beside him through the night, talking to him all the while. At dawn, she carried Rontu to the cliff, urging him to bark at the seagulls as he had always done. But Rontu could not bark, and he silently dropped at Karana's feet and died. Covering him with pebbles of many colors, Karana buried her faithful dog on the headland with sand flowers and a stick that he had fondly chased.

Multiple Choice

Directions:

Circle the letter of the correct answer.

1. After the Aleut ship landed on her island, Karana was mostly afraid that...

   A. the Aleut men would find her and kill her.

   B. the Aleuts would take her back to their country.

   C. the Aleut girl would find her.

2. When Karana discovered that the Aleuts had not brought their dogs, she felt...

   A. unhappy because she wanted a mate for Rontu.

   B. worried because they might take Rontu from her.

   C. relieved because they would have followed Rontu's tracks to the cave.

3. When Tutok asked Karana if she lived in the cave, Karana...

   A. nodded yes.

   B. shook her head and pointed to the far side of the island.

   C. took Tutok to the house on the headland.

4. When Tutok held the cormorant skirt up to her waist, Karana...

   A. decided to give it to her.

   B. snatched it away from her because she hated the Aleuts.

   C. decided to make another skirt for Tutok.

5. Since Tutok and Karana did not speak the same language, they communicated by...

   A. making gestures.

   B. pointing and trading names from each language.

   C. using a common sign language which both tribes knew.

6. When Karana befriended the wounded sea otter left by the hunters, she...

   A. took it home to swim in the ravine.

   B. nursed its wounds and put it out to sea.

   C. put it in a tide pool and fed it fresh fish.

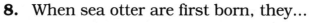

7. Mon-a-nee finally swam out to sea because...

   A. Karana could not feed him when the waves were high.

   B. he didn't like being around humans.

   C. he wanted to join his mate.

8. When sea otter are first born, they...

   A. cannot swim and have to hold on to their mother.

   B. can swim right from the start.

   C. can float but learn to swim from their mothers.

9. When it came time for Rontu to die, he...

   A. lay down by Karana's bed.

   B. went to the lair where he had once lived.

   C. went to the beach where he and Karana had always walked.

10. When Karana buried Rontu, she...

   A. put in a stick he liked to chase.

   B. placed cormorant feathers on his grave.

   C. made a grave marker from sea shells.

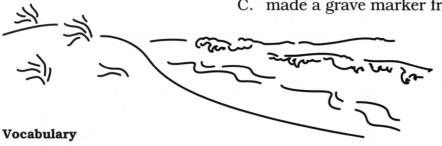

Vocabulary

Directions:

Fill in the blank with

the correct word.

giddy	smelt	reef
prow	fledgling	quiver
reproachfully	teetering	urged

1. _____   a young bird

2. _____   encouraged; pushed or forced

3. _____   silly; light hearted or foolish

4. _____   small fish having oily flesh

5. _____   a case for holding arrows

6. _____   in a scolding manner

7. _____   a ridge of sand or rock just about
                                           even with the surface of the water

8. _____   standing or walking unsteadily

9. _____   the forward part of a boat or ship

Essay Questions

Directions:

Answer in complete

sentences.

1. When Karana first saw the Aleut girl, she could easily have
killed her. Why do you think she chose not to?

_____

_____

_____

_____

_____

_____

2. Karana had a hard life living alone on the island for many
years, but she found ways to make her life happier. Name
three things Karana did to improve her life.

_____

_____

_____

_____

_____

_____

Student Directives

1. Discuss Karana's winter.

2. Tell about Karana's plan to capture Rontu's son.

3. Explain how xuchal helped Karana catch the dog.

4. Briefly describe Rontu-Aru.

5. Discuss Karana's loneliness for Tutok and Ulape.

Vocabulary

glimpse   a brief look

stride (n)   a long step; a manner of walking or running

snares (n)   traps made with a noose

thong   a thin strip of leather used for tying

Summary

The winter after Rontu's death, Karana went out little because of the rain and strong winds. She spent her time making four snares. In the previous summer, Karana had once seen a dog that looked like Rontu's son. She set out to capture the dog using the snares she had made during the winter. When she had no success with the snares, Karana decided to put the toluache weed in the wild dogs' drinking water to sedate them. Discovering that this weed wasn't strong enough, Karana remembered xuchal, a mixture of ground sea shells and tobacco. All the dogs went to sleep after drinking the mixture. Karana found Rontu's son and carried him to her home. He was not as big as Rontu, but he had a thick coat and yellow eyes. She named him Rontu-Aru—Son of Rontu. Though times were happier with the friendship of Rontu-Aru, Karana thought more and more about her sister, Ulape, and Tutok. She missed them very much.

Student Directives

1. Discuss the sweltering summer heat.

2. Describe the tidal wave and its effect on Karana.

3. Describe where Karana took refuge from the tidal waves.

4. Briefly tell about Karana's return to the headland.

5. Describe the earthquake that followed the tidal waves.

Vocabulary

crest — the top of a wave

currents (n) — flows of water

vanquished — those who are defeated in battle

Summary

The sweltering heat of summer came after the fierce winter. The air was so heavy that it was hard to breathe. Because of this, Rontu-Aru had not come with Karana as she worked on the leaks in her canoe. The weather was so stifling that Karana took a nap under the canoe to escape the heat. She was awakened by a rumbling sound in the distance. Looking around her, she thought that she had been transported to another place. Never had the tide been so low, nor the beach so changed. Karana then noticed a cresting wave rumbling toward the island. Terrified, she raced through the rushing waters to the higher land of a cliff where she clung desperately to the rocks until the huge wave spent its fury. No sooner had one giant wave begun to subside than another came crashing down. Suddenly, all was quiet and night came. Karana could not have found her way home at night, so she spent the night crouched under the cliff. When Karana returned to the headland the next day, Rontu-Aru jumped for joy. She slept all day, relieved that no damage had come to the headland. But there was more to come. At dusk that evening as Karana and Rontu-Aru returned from the spring, she suddenly felt the earth move violently. For a moment, she seemed to be standing on air. When Karana and Rontu-Aru were able to get home, they lay all night listening as rocks fell and the earth trembled. By morning, the island was quiet.

Figurative Language, Page 1

Name _____

Scott O'Dell won the Newbery Medal for writing *Island of the Blue Dolphins*. Each year the Newbery Medal is given to an author for excellence in children's literature. In order to merit such an honor, Scott O'Dell had not only to develop a compelling story line but also had to write it exceptionally well. The haunting beauty of *Island of the Blue Dolphins* makes the reader want to continue reading O'Dell's work.

One technique employed by accomplished authors, such as Scott O'Dell, is the use of figurative language in their writing. Figurative language sparks the reader's imagination and makes the story come alive.

You will find that O'Dell uses similes and metaphors in his writing.

Simile: a type of figurative language which uses *like* or *as* to show similarities between two different things. Example: Gentle <u>as</u> a lamb.

Metaphor: a type of figurative language which says that one thing is another. Example: The Lord <u>is</u> my Shepherd.

Directions:
1. Read each figurative expression and discuss how its use enhanced the story. If the expression is a simile, write "simile" next to the expression. If it is a metahpor, write "metaphor."

2. Choose two of your favorite expressions and draw a cartoon for each. Be sure to use the expression in your cartoon.

_____ 1. "He was small for one who had lived so many suns and moons, but quick as a cricket."

_____ 2. "The sea is smooth," Ramo said. "It is a flat stone without any scratches."

_____ 3. "In the morning when he crawls out of his tent he sits on a rock and combs until the beard shines like a cormorant's wing."

_____ 4. "The huts looked like ghosts in the cold light."

_____ 5. "I have never seen the ocean so calm and the sky looks like a blue shell."

Figurative Language, Page 2

Name _____

_____ 6. "There were many hummers which can stand still in the air and look like bits of polished stone..."

_____ 7. "...or the talk of the pelicans which sounds like the quarreling of toothless old men."

_____ 8. "...and as the water lapped against the walls it sounded like the soft music of a flute."

_____ 9. "She was graceful and the skirt flowed around her like water, but I hated the Aleuts and took it from her."

_____ 10. "There was a faint sound as if some giant animal were sucking the air in and in through its teeth."

_____ 11. "Night came, but the earth still rose and fell like a great animal breathing."

Cartoons

Expression Number _____

Expression Number _____

Tsunami

Name _____

In Chapter 27, Karana endured one of nature's most terrifying forces—the dreaded tsunami. As Karana clung desperately to the high rock, she vividly described the tsunami's crash:

"The tongues of water licked into all the crevices, dragged at my hand and at my bare feet gripping the ledge. They rose high above me along the face of the rock, up and up, and then spent themselves against the sky and fell back, hissing past me to join the water rushing on toward the cove." *(P. 173)*

From Karana's frightening description, we can clearly imagine the savage force of the waves.

Tsunami are commonly called tidal waves, but they are not caused by tides at all. A tsunami is actually a large, destructive ocean wave caused by an underwater earthquake or volcano on the ocean floor. We frequently read about earthquakes and volcanic eruptions on land, but they can occur on the ocean floor as well.

Out on the open sea, a tsunami reaches only a few feet in height. When it reaches shallow water, however, the wave becomes tremendous and can reach heights up to 70 feet. The reason the tsunami has such power is because of the great amount of water in the ocean. When the earth shifts on the ocean floor, it affects the sea much as if a great object had been dropped into the water. From the object's drop, a series of concentric waves arise from the center of the disturbance. With such great amounts of water available, great amounts of destructive energy are released.

Directions: After carefully reading the above article on the tsunami, match the terms on the left with the phrases on the right. Place the correct letter on each line.

_____ Tsunami   A. Where the tsunami's force is greatest

_____ Tidal wave   B. Why a tsunami has such force

_____ Underwater earthquake C. Large, destructive ocean wave

_____ Shallow water   D. Height tsunami can reach

_____ 70 feet   E. Incorrect term for tsunami

_____ Amount of ocean water F. Concentric waves arise from this

_____ Center of disturbance G. Causes tsunami

CHAPTER 28
PAGE 176

Student Directives

1. Discuss Karana's losses from the great waves.

2. Tell what Karana used to start building a new canoe.

3. Explain Karana's reaction to the sighting of the ship and to the man who called to her.

4. Relate what Karana did as the men came ashore.

5. Describe Karana's reaction as the ship pulled away.

Vocabulary

uneasy	uncomfortable; nervous
hasten	to hurry; speed up
whence	where; what place or source

Summary

Although the earthquake did little to the island, the great tidal waves had been cruel. The canoes were Karana's greatest loss. Since wood was so scarce, she had to piece together planks from the old canoes. One day while at this difficult task, Karana spotted a ship on the horizon. The ship did not have the red prow of an Aleut ship, nor was it the white men's ship. Karana's first instinct was to hide, but she considered that the men could also have been sent by her people. From her hiding place, Karana heard one man shout when he found her fire and canoe. She knew that he was calling to her, but Karana did not answer the call. Instead, she went back to her house to gather some belongings and to bid good-bye to her island. When Karana returned to the spot where she had heard the man calling, he had left and the ship was leaving the harbor. She shouted to no avail and stood watching until the ship was out of sight.

Character Development

Karana was a remarkable young girl. Having lived all of her life cloaked in the safety and security of her tribal village, Karana had her familiar life cruelly taken from her. With the slaughter of much of her tribe, Karana's peaceful, happy life changed forever. After jumping ship to rescue her brother, Ramo, Karana suffered yet another devastating loss when he, too, was killed. Alone on a deserted island, Karana had to fend for herself against almost insurmountable odds—hunting the wild dogs, finding food for herself, building a shelter, and enduring loneliness.

Scott O'Dell masterfully develops Karana's character through her thoughts, conversations, and actions. With courage and determination, Karana struggled through one obstacle after another in rebuilding her life alone on her island.

Good literature, like *Island of the Blue Dolphins*, serves not only to entertain and educate us, but also to enrich us spiritually. In analyzing Karana's character, not only do we learn about her character development, but we are also given examples of how we can strive to conduct our own lives. Like Karana, we too must develop our own strength of character.

The Discovering Literature Series focuses on ten character virtues:

Responsibility	Friendship
Courage	Persistence
Compassion	Hard Work
Loyalty	Self-discipline
Honesty	Faith

The following pages apply many of these virtues to Karana. Using incidents from the novel, list examples of Karana's virtues.

Character Development, Page 1

Name_____

Directions: Karana portrays a strong, responsible character in *Island of the Blue Dolphins.* Give examples from the novel to illustrate the virtues listed below.

Responsibility

_____

_____

_____

_____

Courage

_____

_____

_____

_____

Compassion

_____

_____

_____

_____

Loyalty

_____

_____

_____

_____

Friendship

_____

_____

_____

_____

Character Development, Page 2

Name _____

Persistence

_____

_____

_____

_____

Hard Work

_____

_____

_____

_____

Self-discipline

_____

_____

_____

_____

Can you think of other qualities that Karana possessed? Give examples.

_____   _____

_____

_____

_____   _____

_____

_____

Which of Karana's virtues would you like to imitate? Why?

_____

_____

_____

_____

Student Directives

1. Tell when the ship finally returned.

2. Describe Karana's actions when she knew she would be rescued.

3. Briefly describe the short man who found Karana and her reactions to him.

4. Relate what Karana learned at Mission Santa Barbara.

5. Describe Karana's feelings at leaving the island.

Vocabulary

ornament   a decoration of beauty

Summary

Two years later, the ship returned to Karana's island. Before greeting the men, Karana bathed in the spring and dressed in her best clothes, even marking a blue and white design on her face to indicate that she was unmarried. Karana made a final meal for herself and Rontu-Aru, but she was unable to eat it. Three men came ashore to greet her. The short one wore a string of beads around his neck. Karana wanted to laugh at the strange words he spoke, but she soon became accustomed to the beautiful sounds of his human voice. She communicated with gestures and agreed to go on the ship with the men, taking her birds and Rontu-Aru. Before the ship left, the men made a blue dress for Karana. Although she did not like the hot, scratchy dress, Karana wore it, smiling as she put her cormorant skirt in her basket. Karana wanted to know more about the ship that had taken her people away years before. The men did not understand her. Not until she arrived at Mission Santa Barbara did she learn that the ship had sunk in a great storm after it reached the mainland. As Karana left the Island of the Blue Dolphins, she thought of all the happy days she had spent there with Rontu, her birds, and the dolphins leaping in and out of the sea.

Plot Development

Authors must plan for three major elements—characters, setting, and plot—when creating a story. Of the three narrative elements, plot is usually the most difficult to develop.

In every well-developed plot, the central character has a problem, or conflict, to overcome. The central problem can be a conflict between two people, between a character and the society in which she or he lives, between a character and nature, or it could even be a conflict within the main character. Whatever the conflict, the main character works through his or her problem throughout the novel or script. In doing so, the main character encounters a series of minor problems, or difficulties; however, these are all directed toward resolving the major conflict.

The structure of a plot can be compared to climbing a mountain. At the base of the mountain, the reader is introduced to the main characters and to the setting. The story develops and the reader is presented with a major problem to be overcome. All the while, the reader is steadily climbing the mountain until he or she reaches the peak, where the action reaches a high point or climax. As soon as the climax has been reached, the action falls rapidly—just as a skier would when rushing down the back side of a snowy mountain. Once the action falls, the reader sees the central character resolve her or his problem.

The Plot Organization Map graphically illustrates how the plot is developed. Using the following Rising Action topics and Falling Action topics, complete the Plot Organization Map. Plot the events sequentially and fill in the characters, setting, problem, and resolution.

Duplicate the Plot Organization Map on oversize paper for ease of use.

Rising Action

•Karana builds house.

•Aleuts slaughter natives.

•Karana is rescued.

•Karana befriends Rontu.

•Karana attempts escape.

•Karana makes weapons.

•Karana faces nature's fury.

•Karana is stranded.

•Karana befriends Tutok.

•Karana misses ship.

Falling Action

•Karana goes to mission.

•Karana learns about ship.

Name _____

Plot Organization Map

Turning Point

Karana faces nature's fury.

Falling Action

Rising Action

Karana makes weapons.

Karana is stranded.

Characters

Setting

Problem

Resolution

Multiple Choice

Directions:

Circle the letter of the

correct answer.

1. Karana was finally successful in capturing Rontu's son when she...

    A. used her snares baited with fish.

    B. put the toluache weed into the dogs' drinking water.

    C. put xuchal, a mixture of ground sea shells and tobacco, into the dogs' water.

2. Karana filled the cracks in her canoe with...

    A. a clay mixture.

    B. pitch.

    C. a type of cement.

3. The rumbling sound that Karana heard on the last sweltering summer day was...

    A. thunder and lightning.

    B. a huge tidal wave.

    C. an explosion.

4. After the giant waves had rushed back to sea, Karana...

    A. spent the night at the foot of the cliff.

    B. raced home to be with Rontu-Aru.

    C. spent the night on the cliff where she had run for safety.

5. The disaster which struck the night after the tidal waves was...

    A. a fierce hurricane.

    B. a violent tornado.

    C. a terrifying earthquake.

6. After the disaster, Karana's greatest loss was the...

    A. damage to her house and fence.

    B. loss of her canoes.

    C. loss of all the food and weapons stored in the cave.

7. To get a new canoe, Karana had to...

    A. piece together the planks of wrecked canoes.

    B. look for wood on the island to build another one.

    C. find one hidden in the cave.

8. Karana could tell that the ship approaching the harbor did not belong to the Aleuts because it...

    A. had a different type of sail than the Aleut ship.

    B. did not have a red, beaked prow.

    C. bore a different symbol than the Aleut ship.

9. When the man from the first ship called out to Karana, she...

    A. raced to the beach to meet him.

    B. hid in her cave.

    C. went back to her house to gather her belongings.

10. Karana learned at Mission Santa Barbara that her people had not come for her because...

    A. the people were afraid to return.

    B. their ship had sunk in a great storm soon after reaching Santa Barbara.

    C. their ship had sailed far off its course.

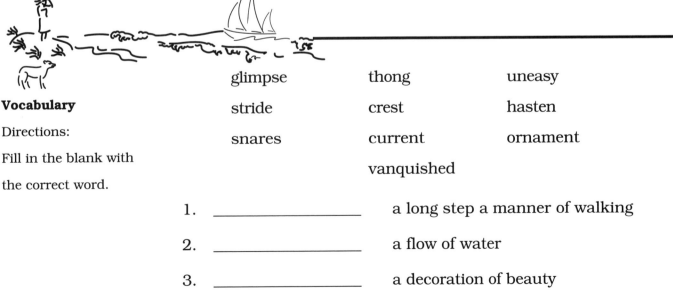

Vocabulary

Directions:

Fill in the blank with

the correct word.

glimpse   thong   uneasy

stride   crest   hasten

snares   current   ornament

vanquished

1. _____ a long step a manner of walking

2. _____ a flow of water

3. _____ a decoration of beauty

4. _____   a thin strip of leather used for tying

5. _____   a brief look

6. _____   the top of a wave

7. _____   uncomfortable; nervous

8. _____   traps made with a noose

9. _____   those who are defeated in battle

10. _____   to hurry

Essay Questions

Directions:

Answer in complete

sentences.

1. Karana lived many years alone on her island. When it finally came time for her rescue, she had mixed feelings about leaving. Give details from the novel which support this statement.

_____

_____

_____

_____

_____

2. When her rescuers questioned Karana about the whereabouts of the sea otter, Karana pretended not to understand. Why did she behave this way?

_____

_____

_____

_____

_____

Directions: Use the Writer's Forum at the end of the novel or after each appropriate chapter.

1. Pretend that you are Karana and write a journal entry about a part of the novel which appeals to you. (Suggestions: choosing a home site by the sea elephants [Chapter 11], taming Rontu [Chapter 15], killing the devilfish [Chapter 19], befriending Tutok [Chapter 21-22]).

2. Pretend that you are an investigative reporter sent to interview Karana at Mission Santa Barbara after her rescue. List the questions you would ask Karana, as well as her responses. Remember to ask the "reporter questions"—who, what, when, where, why, and how. (End of novel)

3. Research and make diagrams of the sea life mentioned in the novel:

gulls   abalones
smelt   sea otter
dolphins   sea elephants
octopus   white bass

4. Karana encountered Tutok near the mouth of the cave where she had been hiding from the Aleuts. At first, Karana thought about attacking Tutok, but she decided to make friends with her instead. Write about a time when you made a new friend. What were your impressions? Fears? Hopes? (After Chapter 22)

5. Write a newspaper account of Karana's rescue by the missionaries. Remember to answer the reporter questions in your article. (End of novel)

6. Karana could easily have given in to despair after she endured nature's wrath from the tidal waves and the earthquake. The great waves cost her all her food and weapons, as well as the loss of her canoes. Write a letter to Karana commending her for her courage and perseverance in the face of her great losses. (After Chapter 28)

WRITER'S
FORUM

Island of
the Blue
Dolphins

Page 2   Name _____

7. Karana chose Rontu for a pet—a companion to ease her loneliness. Write about a favorite pet of yours or one that you know of. Describe the pet, and explain the enjoyment received from it.   (After Chapter 15)

8. Karana had a frightening adventure when she and Rontu explored the Black Cave. Tell about an experience from your life when your spirit of adventure caused you to be afraid. (After Chapter 20)

9. After many years of solitude on her island, Karana finally spotted a ship which did not belong to the Aleuts. When one of the men from the ship discovered Karana's fire and called to her, she hesitated. Instead of rushing out to greet the man, Karana seemed undecided about what she should do. Write about a time when you had a big decision to make and your different feelings about it.   (After Chapter 28)

Chapter Title _____   Name _____

Chapter Summary: _____

_____

_____

_____

_____

_____

_____

_____

_____

_____

_____

_____

_____

_____

_____

Chapter Vocabulary:

1. _____

_____

2. _____

_____

3. _____

_____

4. _____

_____

NAME: _____

Island of the Blue Dolphins

Island of the Blue Dolphins

Skill Page: Setting of *Island....* Page 9.

<u>C</u> San Nicolas Island

<u>A</u> California

<u>B</u> Aleutian Islands

<u>F</u> Russians

<u>D</u> Alaska

<u>E</u> United States

Skill Page: Outlining. Page 10.

I. Setting

 A. Where

  1. Island 20 leagues from Santa Barbara, CA

  2. Found in Pacific Ocean

 B. Sea Life

  1. Whales

  2. Dolphins

  3. Gulls

  4. Cormorants

  5. Sea otter

 C. Land Forms/Vegetation

  1. Roots

  2. Heavy brush

  3. Toyon bushes

  4. Many rocks

 D. land Animals

  1. Crickets

  2. Lizards

II. Characters

 A. Karana

  1. Serious

  2. Observant

  3. 12 years old

 B. Ramo

  1. Imaginative

  2. Playful

  3. 6 years old

 C. Chief Chowig

  1. Chief of Ghalas-at

  2. Remembered another hunt

  3. Wanted to divide catch equally

 D. Captain Orlov

  1. Looked at harbor as if it were his

  2. Claimed to come in peace

  3. Came to hunt sea otter

  4. Wanted to camp on island

  5. Did not want to divide catch equally

Test: Chapters 1-5. Page 16.

Multiple Choice

1. C	6. C
2. B	7. C
3. C	8. A
4. A	9. B
5. B	10. C

Vocabulary

1. ceased	6. stalked
2. kelp	7. parley
3. league	8. stunted
4. mesa	9. portioned
5. ravine	10. pelt

Essay Questions

1. The island on which Karana lived was shaped somewhat like a dolphin, and many dolphins lived in the sea surrounding the island. P. 16-17.

2. The Aleut tribe had hunted on the island before and had not been fair to the villagers. P. 14.

 Captain Orlov only reluctantly agreed to share equally with the villagers. P. 15.

 Captain Orlov looked at the harbor as if it were his. P. 12.

3. When Chief Chowig told Captain Orlov his secret name, the villagers felt he had weakened himself and that was the reason he had been killed. P. 13, 31.

   Accept reasonable answers.

Skill Page: About the Characters. Page 21.

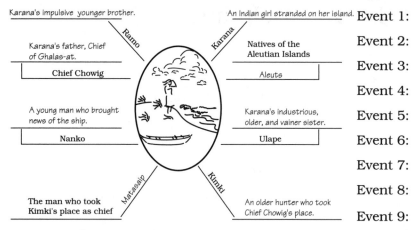

Karana's impulsive younger brother. — **Ramo**

An Indian girl stranded on her island. — **Karana**

Karana's father, Chief of Ghalas-at. — **Chief Chowig**

Natives of the Aleutian Islands — **Aleuts**

A young man who brought news of the ship. — **Nanko**

Karana's industrious, older, and vainer sister. — **Ulape**

The man who took Kimki's place as chief — **Mataasip**

An older hunter who took Chief Chowig's place. — **Kimki**

Skill Page: Elements of a Narrative. Page 25.

Main Character

A. Karana was responsible. She gathered food for her family and took care of her younger brother, Ramo. She made sure that he had enough food to eat and kept him from dangerous situations.

B. Karana was courageous. When the ship was sailing away in the rough seas, she jumped off to protect Ramo, who had been left stranded on the island.

C. Karana was well disciplined. After the wild dogs killed Ramo, she could have given in to despair; instead, she resolved to kill off the wild dogs.

Setting

A. Where: Pacific island shaped like a dolphin.

B. When: In the 1800s.

Plot

A. Karana is an Indian girl who lives a happy, natural life on a Pacific island with other members of her tribe.

B. The islanders' enemies are the Russians and the Aleuts, who cheat Karana's tribe out of the payment for sea otter pelts.

C. Captain Orlov and the Aleuts kill off many of Karana's tribe, including her father.

D. Karana is left stranded on the island after she jumps ship to protect her brother, Ramo.

E. Karana will have to overcome many obstacles to survive alone on the island, but she will ultimately be saved.

Accept reasonable answers.

Skill Page: Sequencing. Page 27.

Event 1:   Children spot Aleut ship.

Event 2:   Argument about dividing catch.

Event 3:   Sea otter slaughtered.

Event 4:   Captain Orlov leaves without paying.

Event 5:   Aleuts and islanders battle.

Event 6:   Kimki elected new chief.

Event 7:   White men's ship arrives.

Event 8:   Ramo runs to get spear.

Event 9:   Karana jumps from ship.

Event 10: Ramo killed by wild dogs.

Event 11: Karana makes weapons.

Event 12: Karana tries to flee.

Test: Chapters 6-10. Page 28.

Multiple Choice

1. B	6. B
2. C	7. C
3. B	8. A
4. A	9. A
5. C	10. C

Vocabulary

1. befell	6. strode
2. forlorn	7. crevice
3. omen	8. gorged
4. ponder	9. beckoned
5. chafing	10. dune

Essay Question

Chief Chowig gave his secret name to Captain Orlov. The Chief's people believed that his death resulted from the weakening of his power from telling his secret name. P. 31.

Karana's tribe forbade women from making weapons. They believed that the four winds would blow and smother the woman, or the earth would tremble and bury her. P. 61.

On her return to the island, Karana saw dolphins, which made her happy. They were believed to be animals of good omen. P. 73.

Accept reasonable answers.

Skill Page: Cause and Effect. Page 32.

1. F	6. A
2. H	7. I
3. J	8. G
4. C	9. B
5. D	10. E

Test: Chapters 11-15. Page 37.

Multiple Choice

1. C	6. B
2. B	7. B
3. C	8. A
4. A	9. B
5. C	10. C

Vocabulary

1. grating	6. clamor
2. carcass	7. lobe
3. rival	8. wary
4. brackish	9. gruel
5. venturing	10. bolder

Essay Questions

1. Karana wisely chose a spot to build her house. • Karana built her fence from whale bones. • Karana gathered food for storage. • Karana began making weapons. • Karana found teeth from a dead bull sea elephant. • Karana lived near the sea elephants, which were amusing to watch. • Karana smoked out the wild dogs from their lair.

2. (Inference). Karana may have thought the dog's intelligence would make him a valuable friend. • Karana may have wanted to weaken the dogs' power by taking their leader from them. • Karana may have liked the dog's size and power. • Karana may have thought that the dog was used to people, since he was an Aleut dog.

Accept reasonable answers.

Test: Chapters 16-20. Page 45.

Multiple Choice

1. C	6. C
2. B	7. B
3. C	8. C
4. A	9. A
5. B	10. C

Vocabulary

1. haunches	6. singed
2. flailing	7. barbed
3. devilfish	8. shaft
4. prey	9. lure
5. roost	10. heed

Essay Questions

1. Karana knew that if she intervened, the dogs would come back after Rontu. She was worried that Rontu would find himself in less favorable circumstances the next time.

2. Karana struggled with the devilfish while it was in the water. The string attached to her spear pulled on her hands until they bled. When the devilfish finally slid up onto the sand bar, Rontu sank his jaws into its body, but three of the devilfish's arms wrapped around him. Karana, rushing to save Rontu, stabbed the devilfish with her knife.

Accept reasonable answers.

Test: Chapters 21-25. Page 53.

Multiple Choice

1. C	6. C
2. C	7. A
3. B	8. A
4. B	9. B
5. B	10. A

Vocabulary

1. fledgling	6. reproachfully
2. urged	7. reef
3. giddy	8. teetering
4. smelt	9. prow
5. quiver	

Essay Questions

1. Karana was probably curious about seeing another human after living alone so long on the island. She was probably hoping the girl would become her friend.

2. Karana captured Rontu and made him her pet. • Karana captured and tamed two pet birds. • Karana made dress-up clothes and walked the beach with Rontu. • Karana made friends with the Aleut girl. • Karana made friends with the wounded sea otter. • Karana built a comfortable home for herself.

Accept reasonable answers.

Skill Page: Figurative Language. Page 58.

1. simile	7. simile
2. metaphor	8. simile
3. simile	9. simile
4. simile	10. simile
5. simile	11. simile
6. simile	

Skill Page: Tsunami. Page 60.

C   Tsunami

E   Tidal wave

G   Underwater earthquake

A   Shallow water

D   70 feet

B   Amount of ocean water

F   Center of disturbance

Skill Page: Character Development. Page 63.

Possible examples to support virtues.

Responsibility:

1. Karana worked at providing food for her village. Even when she spotted the ship, Karana kept digging for roots.

2. Karana took care of her younger brother, Ramo.

3. Karana felt it was wrong to slaughter so many sea otter, so she talked to her father about stopping it.

Courage:

1. Karana jumped ship to rescue Ramo.

2. Karana vowed to kill the wild dogs that had killed her brother.

3. Karana got the teeth of a bull sea elephant to make weapons.

4. Karana wrestled with the devilfish.

Compassion:

1. Karana felt sadness at seeing the sea otter slaughtered.

2. Karana couldn't leave her brother stranded on the island.

3. Karana cared for Rontu's wounds.

Loyalty:

1. Karana jumped ship to be with Ramo.

2. Karana took good care of Rontu and her birds.

Friendship:

l. Karana talked to her father about the slaughter of the sea otter, her friends.

2. Karana befriended Rontu, and the two became inseparable.

3. Karana befriended Tutok even though she was an Aleut.

4. After becoming friends with Won-a-nee and her babies, Karana did not kill any more sea otter or other animals.

Persistence:

1. Karana did not give up when Ramo was killed.

2. Karana decided to paddle to the country which lay to the east.

3. Karana built a fence and house.

Hard Work:

l. Karana worked hard at gathering food.

2. Karana built a fence from whale ribs and bull kelp.

3. Karana painstakingly gathered wood for her house.

4. Karana rebuilt her canoe after the tsunami's devastation.

Self-discipline:

1. Karana did not despair after Ramo's death, but she vowed to kill the wild dogs.

2. Karana felt happy to return to the island after her failed canoe escape.

3. Karana kept going for many years alone on the island.

4. Karana did not despair after Rontu's death; she captured his son instead.

5. Karana did not despair after the terrible destruction from the tsunami and earthquake.

Accept reasonable answers.

Skill Page: Plot Development. Page 67.

Name ___Key___

Plot Organization Map

Labels on the plot diagram:
- Aleuts slaughter natives.
- Karana is stranded.
- Karana attempts escape.
- Karana builds house.
- Karana makes weapons.
- Karana befriends Rontu.
- Karana befriends Tutok.
- Karana misses ship.
- Karana faces nature's fury.
- Karana is rescued.
- Rising Action
- Turning Point
- Falling Action
- Karana goes to mission.
- Karana learns about ship.

Characters
Karana
Chief Chowig
Captain Orlov
Ramo
Tutok
Rontu
Missionaries
Islanders

Setting
Island in the Pacific Ocean

Problem
Karana must survive the elements, the wild dogs, and loneliness on her island until a ship rescues her.

Resolution
After many years alone on the island, Karana is finally rescued by missionaries.

Test: Chapters 26-29. Page 68.

Multiple Choice

1. C	6. B
2. B	7. A
3. B	8. B
4. A	9. C
5. C	10. B

Vocabulary

1. stride	6. crest
2. current	7. uneasy
3. ornament	8. snare
4. thong	9. vanquished
5. glimpse	10. hasten

Essay Questions

1. Karana took her time going to meet her rescuers, rather than rushing out to greet them. She showed happiness by bathing in the ravine and dressing in her best clothes. Karana showed that she was willing to adapt to the white men's culture by wearing the uncomfortable dress that her rescuers had made for her. She had thoughts only of the happy times on the island as she was sailing away.

2. Karana did not want the men to kill any more sea otter. The island's animals were her only friends, and she wanted to protect them.

   Accept reasonable answers.